BECOMING GOD

PRAISE FOR *BECOMING GOD*

"*Becoming God* is one of those rare mystical jewels that enchants the soul. A perfect book to read on days when you are in need of grace."

Caroline Myss,
author of *Anatomy of the Spirit* and *Entering the Castle*

"In *Becoming God*, Andrew Harvey's stunning selections of the words of Western mystic Angelus Silesius heartwarmingly reverberate with the ecstasy of Hafiz and Rumi and transport us into 'the abyss of God.' That abyss is not for the faint of heart, yet it is the soul's true north, even as we shudder and shuffle through our resistance until finally proclaiming: Where else would any seeker of God want to be?"

Carolyn Baker,
co-author with Andrew Harvey of *Savage Grace* and
Return to Joy and author of *Collapsing Consciously:
Transformative Truths for Turbulent Times.*

"One of the simplest and most straightforward maps to realizing divine embodiment. A must read in these times steeped with confusion and perplexity."

Banafsheh Sayyad,
dancer, choreographer, founder, Dance of Oneness®

"With these brilliant translations, Andrew Harvey brings us to the doorway of great wisdom. And then he generously invites us in. Once inside, we are reminded of that which we have most deeply forgotten — our inherent divinity. In its absence, we are fractured and lost on life's pathways. We can't help but walk in the wrong direction. In its remembrance, we come back into life with great reverence. Our sacred purpose is ignited. Our path comes clear. In these troubled times, this profound offering calls us home!"

Jeff Brown,
author of *Grounded Spirituality* and *An Uncommon Bond*

"If you had noticed that the fingers pointing at the moon were obviously not the moon … and yet that moonlight had outshone your mind, releasing it into the whole intelligent body and heart … and if you had then taken a deep breath … and if the true, unspeakable, radical, invisible, all-pervading Divine mystery had melted its heart into your heart … then, maybe you would speak like the luminous Angelus Silesius, translated by the astonishing white-hot Andrew Harvey. Discover a poetry that is able to speak the radiant simplicity on the other side of complexity. These poems will startle you to joy and wonder and transparency. And you will be glad."

Terry Patten,
author of *New Republic of the Heart*

"Andrew is a mystical scholar without peer in the world today. No one I know has such a range of passionate interest in all the mystics east and west, ancient and modern, whatever their charism and insight. Andrew loves them all, and with each mystic he shines ever more lucidly with his own deepening intimacy with the Mother. Andrew's reflection of Angelus Silesius is like a brilliant diamond reflecting pure light."

Jim Garrison, PhD,
President, Ubiquity University

"In *Becoming God*, Andrew Harvey takes us deeply and joyfully into an intimate encounter with the oldest mystery of all: how do we define God? How do we measure what God is and isn't? Where do we fit into this relationship? These 108 epigrams invite us into a kind of mystical bellows of folding in and breathing out, inhaling imagery, exhaling gnosis, catching us gently in the pomposity of all our God game-playing and bringing us back clearer and steadier. A perfect companion to *Turn Me to Gold*, this little volume is a trove of stunning insights and wise counsel. It's a book to be sipped and read again and again."

Ellen Gunter,
author of *Earth Calling: a Climate Change Handbook
for the 21ˢᵗ Century*

"To hear the words of that neglected visionary, Angelus Silesius, translated directly from the German by Andrew Harvey — what a gift and what a blessing!"

Anne Baring PhD,
author of *The Dream of the Cosmos: a Quest for the Soul*

"Like the exquisite mystical poetry of Kabir and Rumi, *Becoming God* is an essential addition to the book collection of every mystic. Andrew Harvey captures the vastness, simplicity and depth of 17ᵗʰ-century Christian mystic Angelus Silesius's exalted poems, each opening a window into the mysterious heart of God, each an ecstatic glimpse of the unfathomable intelligence of the Divine. You will want to savor every morsel of this minimalistic, yet rapturous, heavenly feast."

Brad Laughlin,
spiritual teacher and author

"Who better to translate and convey the inner truths of these sacred revelations than Andrew Harvey, the most illumined and perceptive of those writing and speaking of mystical awareness today. Andrew writes as one who has breathed the fire, known the touch of divine presence, and experienced its transfiguration in every pore and corpuscle of his body. Thus, when he encounters a 17th-century mystic such as Angelus Silesius, it is brother speaking to brother, spiritual embodiment acknowledging parallel embodiment, for each has undergone the divine alchemy that only those so transformed can know. He is our own divine messenger, the fiery prophet bringing down eternal truths for our time. Angelus Silesius saw with his inner eye that which was invisible to those who saw only outer phenomena. Likewise, Andrew bestows upon us the gift of inner knowing, for our salvation and ongoing transformation as we too, 'become God'."

Dorothy Walters, PhD,
author of *The Kundalini Poems* and *Some Kiss We Want*

"Andrew Harvey's vast and comprehensive mystical knowledge backlights the simple and profound understanding of meeting the Beloved. In this new set of translations, he offers the testament of seventeenth-century German mystic, Angelus Silesius. These divinely-inspired couplets and sparse stanzas, organized brilliantly into four movements, take us humbly, grandly, and inexorably closer to that union. Silesius is the soil, the seed, and the blossoming of God in himself. 'I was God's already'; yes, he is 'Godded' and we can taste it. Our dark and outrageous humanity is there, yet reading these illumined translations allows us to intimate at the deepest level that 'Heaven is inside us' too. Now I understand why Andrew sees Silesius as one of a glittering handful of universal mystics who can light the way to our next stage of embodied divinity. Personally, the poems opened me in a way so that I could feel union was realizable in my own life. In the end there is no-thing and no knowing but this. Come in. Enter this surprisingly precise placeless place. What awaits you? 'A wandering tent housing eternal majesty'."

Jenny D'Angelo,
poet, author of *Connect with Your Angels*

"My heartfelt gratitude to Andrew Harvey for discovering and revealing this treasure of mystical truth from a Christian source. *Becoming God* challenges us – in simple Alexandrian couplets – to really inquire and embody a direct and transparent experience of who we really *are*. Andrew Harvey invites us to explore and to absorb his contemporary versions of these remarkable ecstatic poems of a 17th-century Catholic priest, physician and mystic – Angelus Silesius. These direct and intimate conversations with God as Oneself offer direct transmissions of the perennial wisdom, dispensed in short and potent outbursts of non-dual medicine for the soul. *Becoming God* invites us to be *just that*. In the words of one of India's greatest woman saints, Anandamayi (1896-1982), '*to see and to hear That which once heard, the desire to see or to hear anything else, disappears forever*'. *Becoming God* awakens the inner music of the human spirit. It is like a distillation of all the wild transmissions of Rumi, Kabir, and Hafiz, Hildegarde von Bingen, John O'Donohue, William Stafford, Sappho, Thunder Perfect Mind, and more, into one radical cooking pot of deep listening. Most essential, *Becoming God*, brings me home – after long years of exploring the ancient mystics of Asia and the Middle East, into the transparent truth of my own mystical Christian backyard, to celebrate communion once more with Love's presence and absence, and the dynamic silence between and beyond all form. *Becoming God* is a revelatory call to us all, to wake up now to the essential truth and wisdom of *who we are*."

Chloe Goodchild,
author of *The Naked Voice, Transform Your Life through the Power of Sound*

BECOMING GOD

108 EPIGRAMS
FROM
THE CHERUBINIC PILGRIM
BY ANGELUS SILESIUS

TRANSLATED BY
ANDREW HARVEY

BECOMING GOD
108 EPIGRAMS FROM THE *CHERUBINIC PILGRIM* BY
ANGELUS SILESIUS TRANSLATED BY ANDREW HARVEY

iUniverse books may be ordered through booksellers or by contacting:

iUniverse
1663 Liberty Drive
Bloomington, IN 47403
www.iuniverse.com
1-800-Authors (1-800-288-4677)

ISBN: 978-1-5320-7631-2 (sc)
ISBN: 978-1-5320-7632-9 (e)

Print information available on the last page.

iUniverse rev. date: 06/12/2019

For Caroline Myss

Beloved soul-sister,
Wisdom's servant

"Blessed and precious beyond price are the friends who dare
to accompany us as we struggle on the hard path to truth."

- Richard of St. Victor

CONTENTS

Forewords. xv

Epigrams xxv

Movement I   As Vast as God 1

Movement II   Heaven Is Inside You. 27

Movement III   Melted in God's Fire 51

Movement IV   From Light to Light 79

The Life of "Angelus Silesius". 111

A Brief History of the Reception of The Cherubinic Pilgrim 119

Acknowledgements. 121

FOREWORDS

God, whose love and joy
are present everywhere,
can't come to visit you
unless you aren't there.

When I first discovered this passage, I slipped it into my pocket and
have carried it with me ever since. Sometimes I reach in and rub the
words between my fingers. God's love and joy are everywhere! Always!
I just need to stay out of my own way. To my surprise, while I have
quoted the aphorism many times both in talks and in writing its author,
17th-century Christian mystic Angelus Silesius, has remained generally
obscure. I thought he was my own little secret.

And so when Andrew Harvey asked if I might consider offering a
small foreword to his revolutionary new translation of Silesius's poetic
masterpiece, *The Cherubinic Pilgrim,* my heart leapt. Now at last,
through the lucid lens of Harvey's own mystical heart, Angelus Silesius
is bound to emerge from the shadows and sing again, opening the
hearts and expanding the consciousness of a whole new generation of
seekers.

That's what happened with the great Sufi master Mevlana Jalaluddin
Rumi, one of the most beloved poets in America. This was not always
so. When I first encountered Rumi as a teenager studying Sufism, there

were only a couple of existing translations in English and these were rather stuffy, accessible only to those with patience for arcane poetics or who, like me, were hungry enough for the spiritual wisdom of the medieval Sufi master that we would take it in any form we could get our hands on. Then a wave of insightful new translators washed onto the shores of America, Andrew Harvey among them, and suddenly Rumi was like a gorgeous genie released from a bottle. He spilled forth and infused the world with beauty and truth, striking the exact chord our souls thirsted for.

It's Angelus Silesius's turn to break us open and quiet our minds and unfurl our soul wings. Silesius, though rooted in the Christian tradition, speaks a universal love language that transcends religious identification and evokes the perennial yearning for union with the Absolute. The wellspring of his wisdom, as you saw in the opening poem, is paradox. He uses language to transcend language, evoking the ineffable sacred state his poems point to. Listen to this one:

Friend, if you want
To express
Eternity's essence
You'll have to
Forget all words.

Angelus Silesius was a German aristocrat who abdicated power and privilege and gave himself over to a life of voluntary simplicity, contemplative prayer, and passionate pursuit of the Real. Silesius is the quintessential non-dual teacher, wrapped in the heart of a lover. The aphoristic quality of his poetry peels away self-indulgent spiritual inclinations and invites us into a naked encounter with the object of our heart's deepest longing: Love Itself. The union Silesius celebrates requires nothing less than the eradication of all our cherished notions of God so that we may have the possibility of a direct experience of the Godhead. He is both rigorous and voluptuous, simultaneously ecstatic and sober.

Godhead is my sap: What greens and blooms from me
Springs from His holy spirit, the force of flowering.

In this vibrant new volume of Silesius's most luminous jewels, you will find the treasure you may not have even known you were seeking. Slow to a stop. Sit quietly with each poem as a meditation, as living prayer. Dissolve into the radiance of these words and remember who you are: a pilgrim, an angel, a being continuously transmuted by the flames of suffering into an intimate friend of the One.

You are loved by all things—
Like a crowd
They hurry toward you
Eager to reach God.

— Mirabai Starr

I have long been allured to the work of Angelus Silesius and especially to this book, *Becoming God*. Reading these selections and translations by Andrew Harvey excites me all over again—and it should excite all of us. Why is that?

First, because our times call for some radical realignment of our modes of thinking and imagining—a stretching of our boundaries and consciousness if you will. If you believe that the modern era, with its emphasis on materialism and so-called "objectivity" that numbers promise is humming along just fine, then this book is not for you. I wouldn't waste your time with it. It will taste like nonsense.

But if you feel that the thought patterns and structures that have dominated our thinking and our institutions for several centuries are failing us deeply, and that interconnectivity and interdependence are the stuff of the universe, then this book is for you. Why is that? Because Angelus Silesius is special in his succinct, almost haiku-like enunciations of the deepest aspects of human experience and the human soul. He takes us to profound places where other authentic mystics take us, to places of darkness and ignorance—notice how the very first page strips us of all we thought we knew about "God" or "Deity"—piercing our smugness about God. Silesius's apophatic divinity hits us in the very first poem that opens this book. Clearly, we are on a journey to deconstruct and dismantle our God talk here. We are journeying into lesser traveled territory. This is what mystics do for us—they take us on adventures too seldom dared.

Another dimension to reading Silesius is to appreciate how deeply a part of the mystical tradition he is. He is not standing alone in his insights and language and the many images he offers us. He is steeped in a lineage, a tradition of creation spirituality mystics.

I first encountered Silesius when I was studying and teaching Meister Eckhart and I recognized in him a kind of poet rendering Eckhart's teachings into poetry or as I said above, haikus. "Live like the rose who lives without a why" he counsels us. Eckhart frequently urges us to live without a why. But it is not only Eckhart who comes alive in these pages—Mechtild of Magdeburg is present ("melted in God's fire"; "the bird in the air, the fish in the water, my spirit in God's hand", etc.); Julian of Norwich ("Everything God created is so small…only a dot"); Thomas Aquinas ("In God all is God"); Jacob Boehme; and more. One does not have to do an analytical study to determine exactly which mystics Silesius has read and studied in depth (though my guess is all of them since that is what drew him to convert from his Lutheran faith to the Catholic tradition—the appeal that the mystics held for him).

What is most useful is to realize that in reading and tasting Silesius you are encountering the best of Western mysticism in so many respects. His work is a sort of shorthanded encyclopedia of mystical (non-dualist) teachings. He may have had experiences from which he writes without having derived them from the readings of Aquinas, Mechtild, Eckhart, Julian, etc., but how are we to know? And does it matter? The point is that he trusted his experiences and uttered them in poetry. His images echo those around the globe who have undergone similar "one-ing" experiences. Art is the proper language for a mystical experience and Silesius is a carrier of that truth.

His poetry stands by itself; but it is also part of a lineage and it is that lineage of mysticism that has been so sorely lacking in Western education and religion during the modern era. That is what makes this book so exciting! It welcomes back that tradition of intuition and one-ing that we call mysticism so that now we can entertain a full expression of what it is to be human.

The title of this book, *Becoming God*, is a bit daring. And dangerous. One should balance that invitation with another one, "Becoming Human". For there is a danger that some people will read the mystics in an effort to escape their humanity and their bodies and the earth and politics and economics and all the rest that humans must undergo in our efforts to discover our deepest God-self which is inclusive of community. This is surely not what Andrew Harvey has in mind nor what Angelus Silesius had in mind nor Meister Eckhart and other creation centered mystics had in mind in calling us to our Divinity. To become God is also to become more human. When Thomas Aquinas says that "compassion is the fire that Jesus came to set on the earth" or when Rabbi Heschel says that we are to be God's hands of compassion while on earth, both are making the point I am making. "Becoming God" means we become more effective instruments of compassion, builders of justice and justice-based communities.

To "become God" on this earth means that we re-engage in the battles of justice and survival and community but from another level of being, from another perspective. One that derives from our God-self and not from our reptilian brains of fight and flight. Or from an angelic projection that would invite us into airy fairy escapes from our bodies or the earth body or the suffering of both. As Meister Eckhart put it, "a person works in a stable; that person has a breakthrough. What do they do? They return to the stable." We return to our work in the world but working from another perspective, a more divine one, a more interdependent and compassionate one therefore, when we encounter the kind of experiences that Silesius underwent and names for us so brilliantly in these pages.

Let us consider a few of these namings.

Page 2, "It is—I don't know what." To enter the world of "I don't know what" is a deeper world than "I am right and you are wrong." It is a world of unknowing and it can empty the mind so that mind-ful-ness might happen.

Page 6, "The abyss of my spirit cries out incessantly to the abyss of God—which is deeper, tell me?" Eckhart says our souls are as unfathomable and as ineffable as God is and he too talks about the "abyss" that we experience.

Page 10. "I am not outside God, God isn't outside me." Pantheism surely.

Page 10. "I'm his brilliance, I'm His light." The Cosmic Christ who shines not on us but from within all of us.

Page 11. "God is my center...my circle when love melts me into Him." Cf. Aquinas: "The first effect of love is melting."

Page 13. "God's like a spring flowing out constantly into his creation yet staying in himself". Cf. Eckhart: "Creativity flows out but remains within."

Page 14. "Godhead is my sap: What greens and blooms from me spring from His holy spirit, the force of flowering." Cf. Hildegard: God is greening power which is the sap of the Holy Spirit.

Page 17. "That I was born for God is beyond doubt; so you don't need to ask me who my Mother is." Mechtild and Julian both celebrate God as Mother.

These citations are found in just the first 17 pages of this book! Imagine what riches await you as you journey further. One could go on and on. But no need.

The need is for the reader to read these pages with an open heart, continue heart first, not head first. Lead with the heart; the head will follow. The heart will shift things in the head. That is what is needed today—a big shift in our minds, our consciousness, one that begins where the mystics begin—with the heart. That is why Angelus Silesius and the mystical tradition he speaks from and gathers his riches from is so needed today. That is why this book can ignite a revolution in consciousness.

Thank you, Andrew Harvey, for bringing Silesius back to our midst. Back to aliveness! Back to lighting fires.

— *Reverend Dr. Matthew Fox*

My translations of Angelus Silesius were done from the 17th-century German—from the Glatz edition of 1675: Johannis Angeli Silésii, *Cherubinischer Wandersmann* Geistreiche Sinn und Schlussreime zur *Gôttlichen Beschauligkeit Anleitende.* This edition was corrected and re-edited in 1986 by the brilliant scholar, Louise Gnadinger (Manesse, Zürich). It is this edition that I have worked from.

I started to teach myself German at the age of 12, passionate to read in the original Rilke's "Duino Elegies" that I had discovered in French translation. Then, at Sherborne school, when I was 14, I pursued my German studies under the most inspired and exuberant of teachers, Mr. Wilkinson, who made me memorize glowing chunks of Goethe, Heine, and Rückert and opened up for me the depths of the German language and seeded in me a passion for its philosophical and emotional subtleties and lyrical lushness.

Angelus Silesius's six-book mystical masterpiece has 1,676 couplets in it (including a few slightly longer poems such as the one that opens my selection). Over two decades of intermittent work, I translated 800 of them. These initial translations were studiously rhymed, as is the original. When I came to read them two years ago, beginning to plan this book, I was aghast. I found what I had done knotted and clunky, the exact opposite of Silesius's fierce paradoxical directness. I despaired, and burned them all one winter night outside the log cabin I was living in in Arkansas.

A year and a half ago, I was sitting alone on the spare Zen-like deck of a lodge in the Namib desert watching a full moon rise in a star-studded sky over stark mountains. I heard a quiet voice in my head say, "Don't rhyme the Silesius poems. Put them into modern free verse while being accurate to the original." From memory I wrote down twenty of my favorites in this new form and over the course of the next six weeks, I retranslated 500 epigrams. As I worked, I became aware that the passion that I had had for Silesius from my early thirties had been burnished and expanded by all that I had lived through since and been graced to know.

With growing amazement, I found that I was discovering *The Cherubinic Pilgrim* not only as the record of an astonishing awakening that draws, as many scholars have pointed out, on almost all the different modes and approaches to God celebrated in the Christian mystical tradition; even more importantly, it was an account of the greatest and most challenging mystery of all, that of what I have come to call the Transfiguration Process. It is this Process, I believe, that holds the key to the next stage of human evolution and the birth on earth in time of an embodied divine humanity.

This realization revolutionized the way I would present Silesius to a modern audience. The Transfiguration Process is the infinitely mysterious and amazing process that transmutes through grace a human being into a radically embodied divine human being; it is the sublime and explosive secret kept long hidden in the heart of many of the world's major mystical traditions. It was this secret that Shams transmitted to Rumi that inflamed the Shaivite mystics of South India who worshipped the golden dancing Shiva of Chidambaram that Kabir lived and proclaimed, that Kabbalists such as Moses de Leon spoke about in dazzling cryptic imagery, that the Vajrayana mystics pursued in their search for the "Rainbow Body", that western alchemists worked on in their pursuit of the "philosopher's stone". It was this secret that guided the pioneering work of all the greatest modern evolutionary mystics, especially Sri Aurobindo, Teilhard de Chardin, and my soul father, Bede Griffiths, the greatest Christian mystic of the 20th century.

It is this secret—of Transfiguration—that blazes at the heart of the authentic Christ transmission obscured by the cowardice, literalism, and mystical ignorance of the churches created in His name but known and lived by many of the greatest Christian saints, such as San Symeon The Theologian, Seraphim of Sarov, the Curé of Ars, and Father Bede Griffiths himself who lived its miracle consciously in the last five years before his death in 1992. Bede told me, "The Resurrection not only birthed Jesus Christ into light-matter; it seeded that birth potentially in every atom of the matter of the Universe and in the depths of the cellular structure of the human being. The crisis we are living in now—the global dark night—is the birth canal of this secret on a vast scale—the extreme crisis designed to birth an embodied divine humanity. This birth is the true Second Coming, that is not the return of Jesus but the rising of Christ consciousness, embodied and dedicated to the transformation of all human life, in millions of beings."

Father Bede added, "This secret is not only the supreme gift of the Christ to us, it is also known in different mystical traditions." He paused and smiled, "How could any one religion or mystical system claim or contain such a secret? It belongs with its astounding promise to all humanity and the whole creation."

What I have presented then in this four-part mystical symphony, *Becoming God*, are the 108 epigrams from Angelus Silesius that most clearly, powerfully, and universally show how the Transfiguration Process is approached and lived. The God of Angelus Silesius is at once utterly transcendent and utterly immanent, beyond any possible concept, formulation, or dogma, and blazingly alive in a stone, or worm or fly. This is the God that all the mystics of the Transfiguration Process, whatever their religion or tradition, come to connect with in awe, humility, ecstasy and what St. John of the Cross called "unknowing knowing". For such a God, nothing, even the Transfiguration of a fragmented, devastated and deluded humanity into a fully embodied divine humanity graced with divine powers, is impossible.

Do not be deceived by the brevity or seeming, sometimes childlike, simplicity of the epigrams of Angelus Silesius. Each one is a light-borne telegram from super-consciousness. Receive them one by one calmly, slowly, meditatively and allow astounding new vistas of possibility to awaken in your being.

Andrew Harvey
Oak Park, Illinois
Easter, 2019

EPIGRAMS

"The world of God is a world of endless expansion."

— Shams of Tabriz

"The wise see the One flaming in all creation."

— The Shvetashvatara Upanishad

"Let divine passion triumph and rebirth you in yourself."

— Rumi

"I've found God's priceless jewel.
Within my own body."

— Kabir

"My spirit received the gift
of unknowing knowing
all knowledge transcended."

— John of the Cross

"Radiant in His light
we awaken as the Beloved
In every last part of our body."

— *San Symeon, the New Theologian*

"God gives birth to the Son as you, as me, as each one of us. As many beings—as many gods in God. In my soul, God not only gives birth to me as his son, he gives birth to me as himself, and himself as me … I have won back what has always been mine. Here, in my own soul, the greatest of all miracles has taken place—God has returned to God!"

— *Meister Eckhart*

"Body and soul are to be transfigured by the divine life and to participate in the divine consciousness. There is a descent of the spirit into matter and a corresponding ascent by which matter is transformed by the indwelling power of the spirit and the body is transfigured."

— *Bede Griffiths*

MOVEMENT I

AS VAST AS GOD

What God is, no-one knows.
God is neither light, nor spirit
God is not bliss, not unity,
Not what we call "deity."
God is not wisdom, nor reason,
Nor love, nor will, nor goodness.
God is not a thing, nor a nothing,
Nor is God essence.
God is what neither I nor you
Nor any creature can understand
Without becoming what God is.

What is eternity?
Neither "this" nor "that"
Not this moment,
Nor a thing, nor nothing.
It is—I don't know what.

In God all is God: the simplest tiny worm
Is in God as great as a thousand Gods.

Look, everything God created
Is so small—
For God
The whole creation
Is only a dot.

God is in Himself all things—
His own Heaven, His own bliss.
Why then did He create us?
Who'll ever fathom this?

The abyss of my spirit cries out incessantly
To the abyss of God—which is deeper, tell me?

The bird in the air
The stone on the ground
The fish in the water
My spirit in God's hand.

God is an eternal present
That's why
He's present eternally
In me.

God lives in light
No roads lead there;
You'll never see that light
If you don't become it.

I am not outside God
God isn't outside me—
I'm His brilliance
I'm His light:
He's my adornment.

God is my center when I hold Him in me
My circle when love melts me into Him.

I am as rich as God
Not a single dust-speck exists
In which (believe me, friend)
I do not have a share.

God's like a spring
Flowing out constantly
Into His creation
Yet staying in Himself.

Godhead is my sap: What greens and blooms from me
Springs from His holy spirit, the force of flowering.

The drop becomes the sea
When it enters into it
And the soul becomes God
When it drowns in Him.

Absorb yourself
Into the deepest depths
Of God's humility—
You'll be the highest radiance
Of all heavenly sparks.

That I was born of God
Is beyond doubt
So you don't need to ask me
Who my Mother is.

God thinks nothing.
To think He thinks
Is to say
God wavers to and fro
Which isn't His way.

Don't wonder, friend,
Why I love staring
Into nothing—
I must keep turning
Towards my Sun.

Even the consciousness of the Cherubim
Cannot satisfy me—
I want to soar to where
Nothing is known.

I am as vast as God
No place in any world
O miracle
Can contain me.

I am God's child and son
And He's my child too.
How does this come to be
That both are both?

A heart, grounded in God,
And still as He desires
Will be the one
He loves to touch—
The lute He plays upon.

Don't search beyond the seas
For spirit and wisdom.
Nobility of soul flames out
From one-pointed love.

Wherever I turn—
Neither beginning nor end,
Neither center nor circle.

When God unites Himself
With the human
The beginning sees
It has found its end.

MOVEMENT II
HEAVEN IS INSIDE YOU

Everything arises from unity
Everything returns to unity;
As soon as duality appears, however,
Everything drowns in multiplicity.

God is pure no-thing, unstained by "here" or "now."
The more you grasp after God, the more God disappears.

It isn't the world that chains you
You are yourself the world
Your yourself hold yourself prisoner.
What you're searching for
Is already here, in you;
All your anguish springs
From not making it appear.

Heaven's inside you, so is Hell's pain and despair.
What you will and choose is with you everywhere.

Be empty—
Water will spring from you
As from the source
Of eternity.

You hope to sit
By the well of life?
Then first, down here,
Sweat out
The water for your thirst.

An eagle can stare directly
Into the blazing sun
And you, if your heart is pure,
Into the eternal lightning.

God is like a fire
And my heart's the furnace
Where He consumes incessantly
The wood of vanity.

Friend, let the world
Go its willful way;
Its acts are nothing
But a tragic play.

Poor human being, don't stay hypnotized
By the world's colors
And your painful life.
All the creation's beauty
Is only a path
That opens the way
To the Creator's supreme beauty.

Grow beyond yourself
And all creatures—
The Divine nature
Will grip onto you.

God is so great, He'd give
Great gifts to us all—
O that we wretches
Have hearts so small!

A heart that time and space can satisfy
Is ignorant of its own immensity.

God demands nothing of you
Other than that you rest in Him.
Do this, and only this—
Leave Him to do the rest.

When you desire Him
And long to be His child
He's in you already.
It's He
Who inspires your desire.

Open yourself to Him
You'll hear Him in you.
If only you'd grow quiet
And hold to silence—
He'd speak endlessly.

When I plunge
Into the abyss of God
I return again
To where I was
From all eternity.

Friend, if you want
To express
Eternity's essence
You'll have to
Forget all words.

The flaming-out of splendor
That blazes in the night—
Who can see it?
A heart with eyes
In constant vigil.

If God lives, dwell in, and moves
Every single creature
Then why do you keep asking
To know
The path to Heaven?

The rose is without why
It blooms because it blooms—
Doesn't attach to itself,
Doesn't seek to be seen.

What all the saints do
All together
An ordinary human being
Can do too.
Realize this:
All the saints do
Is abandon themselves to God.

Love is the touchstone
That tests the gold
And tells it from mud.
Of nothing it makes something
And turns me to God.

Eat, at dusk, holy sorrow's bread—
You'll find prepared an evening meal
Of boundless joy in God.

MOVEMENT III
MELTED IN GOD'S FIRE

My world's my ocean
God's spirit my captain,
My body the ship
My soul comes home in.

This world's too small
Eternity too narrow,
Where could my soul
Truly expand?

In the sea
All is sea
Even the smallest drop.
So tell me
What holy soul in God
Will not be God?

That soul that knows nothing
And loves nothing
But one unique good
Is naturally the bride
Of the eternal bridegroom.

Nobility
Is to be empty
Open always
To instreaming God.

Become God.
If you want to go to God
God gives Himself
To the one
Who wants to be God with Him
And be what He is.

The soul that longs
To hit God's heart
Must aim
With one eye only
That sees right.

I pray to God with God
Through God and in God—
He's my spirit, my word, my psalm
And all that I can.

I was God's life already
Before I came to be.
That's why He's offered up
All of His life for me.

Before I was me
I was God in God
And can be again
If I die to my me.

God Himself, to live for you, must die:
How can you win His life without dying?

If you can't die joyfully
You've got no will to live;
The life you're hungry for
Only death can give.

Love's like Death—
It kills my senses
Shatters my heart
Takes my spirit out.

No sooner have I been
Melted down in God's fire—
He stamps me with His seal
My essence is His own.

O God, how can this be?
My spirit's nothingness
Burns to consume
Your vast eternity!

The circle's in the point
The seed in the fruit
God in the world.
Wise the being
Who searches for Him
In the smallest things.

God makes no distinctions—
Everything's the same for God;
He's just as present
In the fly as in you.

The rose that today
Your outer eyes see
Has bloomed in God, unchanged
From all eternity.

God attaches the same significance
To frog-croaks as to lark-song.

There's nothing imperfect—
A pebble's just as precious
As a ruby;
The frog as ravishing
As any cherubim.

You are loved by all things—
Like a crowd
They hurry toward you
Eager to reach God.

See in your neighbor
Only God and Christ—
The light that spreads
From Divinity.

It's only the annihilation
Of your being
That soars you free
Of yourself.
The most annihilated
Is the nearest to God.

Leave, God will enter.
Die, you'll live in God.
Be nothing, He'll be in you.
Do nothing, and His will
Will be fulfilled.

Die before you die
If you don't want to die
When death comes. If you don't—
Your disappearance
Will be absolute.

I don't believe in death;
May I die each hour!
Each time I have
I've found
A richer life.

It is when you die
That God becomes your life.
Then you transfigure
Yourself into God.

MOVEMENT IV

FROM LIGHT TO LIGHT

God's my final end; I, His beginning.
He finds His essence in me
I vanish into Him.

You are born from God and die in Christ
And are, by the Holy Spirit, resurrected.

The human abandoned to God
Lives in God's peace—
Traveling, each moment,
Beyond time and space.

What my heart
Loves most about blessedness
Is that it births
From my inmost being
And never goes outside.

If you are Godded
You eat and drink God
(This is always true)
With every bite of bread.

I too am God's child; I too sit at God's right hand.
In me God comes to know His spirit, flesh and blood.

I must be sun and paint with my own rays
The color-free sea of total Godhead.

I abandon myself
To God totally.
If He wants
To make me suffer
I'll smile back to Him
As simply as in joy.

I am neither I nor You:
You are this "I" in me
That's why I give you, my God,
All the glory.

Who lives just one day
In eternity
Grows even older
Than God Himself can be.

Being at peace with yourself
One with God and all beings—
That is peace beyond peace.

I have it from God and God from me
That God's so joyful
And lives without desire.
This He gives to me
And this I give to Him.

O sweet Feast! God alone is the wine,
The food, the table, the music
And the one who serves them all to us.

The soul's like a crystal
Godhead its radiance
The body you live in
A shrine for both.

I am myself eternity
When I abandon time.
Me in God
And God in me
Melt together.

The soul in which God dwells
(O bliss!) will be
A wandering tent, housing
Eternal majesty.

For me, nothing's great but God.
A heart filled with God
Sees even in Heaven
Only a tiny cabin.

I am the Godhead's vessel
Into which It pours itself.
It's also my deep sea
And in Itself enfolds me.

There's still more God
Absorbed in me
Than if a small sponge
Held all the vast sea.

Love, when it's new,
Bubbles like a new wine—
The older and clearer
The more calm and still.

God's the eternal Sun
And I'm one of its rays;
That's why I can call myself
Eternal by nature.

There's not a grain of sand
So insignificant
Nor a point so tiny
Where the wise don't see
God's blazing totality.

God is eternal peace
God doesn't search for
Or desire anything.
Make yourself like that
You'll be like God.

Christ could be born
A thousand times;
If He isn't born in you
Your loss is eternal.

God is my spirit
God is my blood
And flesh and bones—
How could I not be
Completely
Deified in Him?

Go where you can't go
Gaze where there's nothing to see
Listen to silence—
You are where God speaks.

True emptiness
Is like a noble vase
Holding nectar: having it
But not knowing it.

Abandon opens to God.
To leave God too
Is an abandon
Only the very few
Ever understand.

Where's my home? Where I and you can't stay.
Where's the end to where I must go?
Where no end is. Where should I go?
Beyond God, into a desert.

Wherever you are, friend,
Never ever stop—
You must progress ceaselessly
From light to light.

Friend, enough: if you want to read more
Become yourself both book and essence.

THE LIFE OF "ANGELUS
SILESIUS"

"Angelus Silesius", the author of *The Cherubinic Pilgrim (Cherubinischer Wandersmann)*, is the mystical pseudonym of Johannes Scheffler. Scheffler was born in Breslau (now Wrocaw, Poland) in 1624, at the beginning of the Thirty Years War that would go on to ravage Europe.

In the 17th century, Breslau was in the province of Silesia. It belonged to the Hapsburgs as rulers of Bohemia since 1526. The parents of Johannes Scheffler were Lutheran German émigrés; Stanislaus, his father, was elevated to the minor nobility in 1595. Wealthy and irascible, at 62, Stanislaus married a woman from the upper middle classes 38 years younger than himself. Johannes was the first of three children; he had a sister whose name has not come down to us and a brother, Christian, who was mentally unstable.

At the age of 15, in 1639, Johannes found himself an orphan. That same year, he began his studies in the Gymnasium of St. Elizabeth of Breslau.

Breslau had avoided the wholescale massacres and destruction the Thirty Years War had brought to the other regions of Germany. Scheffler was a brilliant pupil, intellectually precocious, restless, introverted but passionate, and already preoccupied, as he would be all his life by spiritual inquiry.

The education Johannes received at the Gymnasium was ideally tailored to nourish a literary vocation. Inspired by Martin Opitz, who had laid down rules for German versification in his widely influential *Buch Von Der Deutschen Poetery* (treatise on German poetry) published in 1624, Scheffler and his fellow students were encouraged to write verse both in Latin and the vernacular. His most important early teacher, Kristoph Koeler, was to write the first biography of Opitz; at 18, in 1642, Scheffler dedicated to Koeler a long poem of 60 verses, his first real opus.

In 1643 Johannes Scheffler left Breslau to pursue studies in medicine at the University of Strasbourg. Studying medicine at that time also required courses on politics, history and law. It was during this period that the young Scheffler discovered the work of the great German mystic, John Tauler, a pupil of Meister Eckhart, Tauler would inspire Johannes with many of the central themes of *The Cherubinic Pilgrim*.

In September, 1644, Scheffler was at the University of Leyden in Holland, one of the most prestigious in Europe. He encountered there both the work of Jacob Boehme, the author of "The Way to Christ", (a crucial inspiration later to Sweden Borg and Blake), and a group of Mennonites who championed a direct relationship with the Divine beyond dogma and beyond any control by religious institutions. Probably in 1645 or 1646, Scheffler left Leyden and went to the university of Padua in Italy. Here he met and absorbed the exuberant, ecstatic Catholicism of the counter-Reformation that made him increasingly disillusioned by the aridity of his Lutheran heritage.

On the 9th of July, 1648, at only 21 years old, Johannes Scheffler received, from the University of Padua the title of Doctor of Medicine and Philosophy. He then returned to Breslau where in 1649, thanks to his brother-in-law, Thobias Brückner, himself a doctor, Johannes obtained a position as Court Physician to the fanatically Lutheran Sylvius Nimrod von Württemburg, ruler of the tiny Silesian Duchy of Öls (now Olesnica in Poland). It was here in Öls that he encountered the most influential friend of his life, Abraham von Franckenberg (1593-1652).

The first published text of Johannes Scheffler was his Funeral elegy for his beloved mentor. This long poem of 112 verses makes it clear that for Scheffler, Von Franckenberg was nothing less than his "spiritual father". Without Von Franckenberg's inspiring influence in fact, as many scholars have written, *The Cherubinic Pilgrim* would never have been either conceived or created. Scheffler describes his friend as being already "clothed while alive with that eternity that is now his" with a heart that "often held itself beyond space and time towards God to contemplate His light and His life." For Scheffler, Von Franckenberg was "three times noble"; through his body "born from noble blood", his spirit "born from God", and his soul "chosen by God for the nobility of his virtues".

Abraham von Franckenberg is now remembered above all as the compiler of the works of Jacob Boehme and his first biographer. As noted, Scheffler had already encountered Boehme's works in Lyden. Von Franckenberg's passion for the ecstatic cobbler's radical system of correspondences between God, humanity and nature, that mixed elements of Kabbalism, neo-Platinism and Paraclesian alchemical theory clearly inflamed his brilliant and devoted pupil, who credited Boehme later with being essential to his being "set on the path to the truth".

Von Franckenberg a was a Silesian aristocrat of ascetic habits and profound mystical experience and convictions who would return to his castle at Königsdorf near Öls from voluntary exile after the Thirty Years War ended. His vision, inspired by Boehme, of a Christianity beyond sectarian divisions had brought him into dangerous conflict both with the fervent Catholicism of the Hapsburg's court and with local Lutheran polemicists, and he lived as a recluse in a few barely furnished rooms of his ancestral home.

Von Franckenberg's library, composed of mystical and esoteric texts and rare alchemical manuscripts, was celebrated all over Europe. In recognition of his pupil's devotion, spiritual sincerity and of the focused intensity of his quest, while he was still alive, Von Franckenberg gave Scheffler a collection of medieval mystical texts that ranged from the works of Methilde of Magdeburg and Gertrude of Hakeborn to those of John Tauler and Heinrich Suso. On his death, Von Franckenberg left Scheffler the rest of his sumptuous library.

From what scholars now know of Johannes Scheffler's reading—and the various streams of mystical thought, devotion and revelation that nourished *The Cherubinic Pilgrim* —this rich and diverse collection must have contained also the works of the Flemish master mystic Ruysbroeck (translated into Latin by the Jesuit Sirius) as well as those of St. John of the Cross, Meister Eckhart, Thomas A. Kempis, and a varied selection of alchemical and occult literature, including a set of the works of Paracelsus. Abraham Von Franckenberg was not only a collector of esoterica; he was also the author of several important works—the *Gemma Mystica* and *Oculus Aeternitatis* (1637) both commentaries on Jacob Boehme—and *Raphael Oder Arzt-Engel* (*Raphael or the Doctor Angel*) published after his death in 1688, which fused together a vision of physical and spiritual healing. He was also, it seems, a gifted poet, and the author of a collection of alchemically inspired mystical epigrams almost nothing of which survives, but which we can safely assume was one of the inspirations for the form and subject matter of *The Cherubinic Pilgrim*.

It wasn't only Abraham Von Franckenberg and his Aladdin's cave of a library that galvanized and inspired Johannes Scheffler; the circle around Von Franckenberg also contained the famous visionary, Daniel Czepko, the author of a massive work of which only 600 epigrams survive *Sexcenta Monodisticha Sapientium*. These epigrams were in the same rhyming Alexandrian form as those of *The Cherubinic Pilgrim* and exalted the indissoluble relationship between the soul and Christ. There is no doubt that Czepko's epigrams profoundly inspired Scheffler when he came to conceive and create his masterpiece.

After Von Franckenberg died, Johannes Scheffler compiled a small anthology of prayers which included some by Gertrude of Hakeborn and other magnificent but half-forgotten medieval masters. Permission to publish this anthology, however, was forbidden by the bigoted Lutheran duke's even more bigoted chaplain, Christophe Freitag. This provoked one of the major crises of Scheffler's life; enraged and embittered, he resigned his court position, returned to Breslau and there on June 12,

1653, in the church of St. Matthew, was received into the Catholic church, adopting the name of Johannes Angelus.

This "conversion", the culmination of years of restless inquiry, mystical turmoil and direct revelation, was undoubtedly the crucial event of Scheffler's life. It continues to surprise and even shock many commentators of his work but it is not hard to explain. The majority of the spiritual authors Johannes admired were Catholic; the contemporary Roman Church was far more open to the wildness and glory of the mystical path than mainstream dogmatic Protestantism. It should not be forgotten, for example, that the protestant Jacob Boehme had been forbidden to write at all by his pastor and that one of his most inspired pupils, Valentin Wiegel, never published his own revelations and ideas; they were discovered only after his death and even then, had to be edited in secret. Besides, Lutheranism in Silesia—as Freitag's reaction to Scheffler's anthology made it clear—was hardening into desiccated dogma, contemptuous and suspicious both of the Catholic mystical tradition with its cult of Mary and the Saints and the emotional extravagance of the dissident Protestant sects. Clearly, Johannes Angelus felt that his own intense, fragile and naturally exalted temperament would be more sustained and protected by the Catholic Church of the Counter Reformation than marooned on the dangerous wilder shores of Protestantism.

After his acceptance into the Catholic church, Johannes Angelus plunged into a three-year retreat accompanied by the second greatest soul friend of his life, the priest Sebastian von Rüstock. Von Rüstock later became the leader of the Catholic party in Silesia and Prince-Bishop of Breslau, and protected Angelus for the rest of his life. It was during this prolonged retreat that *The Cherubinic Pilgrim* was almost certainly gestated; Angelus later claimed that his first book of epigrams was written in a storm of sleepless inspiration that lasted four days.

Although we cannot know exactly when the first five books of *The Cherubinic Pilgrim* were written, we do know when they were published. Under the imprimatur of Sebastian von Rüstock and that of the theological University of Vienna, Johannes Angelus, under the freshly minted pseudonym "Angelus Silesius", published two volumes of poetry in 1657. The first contained five books of epigrams—called *Spiritual Aphorisms and Rhymed Sentences* (*Geistiche Sinn Und Schlussrinne*), which did not become *The Cherubinic Pilgrim* until a sixth and final book was added in 1675 in the Glatz edition. It is this complete and definitive edition that all subsequent editions rely on.

On the 29th of May 1661, Johannes Angelus was ordained as a priest and entered into the order of the minor friars of St. Francis. In 1663, Johannes Angelus then embarked, perhaps egged on by von Rostock, on a ferocious pamphlet writing campaign against his Lutheran opponents. In this campaign he proclaimed—astonishingly—the urgent need to take all rights away from Protestants in Silesia and shamelessly advocated persecution of "heretics" in terms so graphically violent that his pamphlets (he wrote 55 of them) were condemned by no less than Catholic bishops. In 1654, however, Johannes Angelus was rewarded for his extremism by becoming doctor at the court in Vienna of the Catholic Emperor Ferdinand.

The brave and original evolutionary mystic who wrote *The Cherubinic Pilgrim* became then, in the last decades of his life, a fanatical adherent to the exclusive authority of the Catholic Church. When Johannes Angelus published 39 of his most inflammatory pamphlets in his book, *Ecclesiologica*, in 1677, he expressed in the preface his profound regret that Catholics are "now ready to let heretics go calmly to hell rather than angering them with the truth." As if this wasn't enough, when the ban on Catholic public processions was lifted in 1661, partly because of his own incessant urging, the writer of *The Cherubinic Pilgrim* walked melodramatically through the main streets of Breslau carrying a large cross and a banner and wearing a crown of thorns. The master of *The Cherubinic Pilgrim* had changed, in perhaps the most baffling and heart-breaking transformation in religious history, into a tragic *grand guignol* clown.

There are four potential explanations of this collapse of the universal mystical poet of *The Cherubinic Pilgrim* into the Catholic fanatic.

The first is that Johannes Angelus was insufficiently psychologically astute and grounded to avoid the massive and dangerous inflation that as Jung pointed out, and all mystical traditions know, supreme inner experience can engender. His parading around the streets of Breslau dressed up as Christ suggests the possibility of this.

Another explanation might be that Johannes found in the authoritarianism of the Catholic church a safe, eternal mother/father that seemed to heal the wound of being orphaned at 15, with all the sense of life's deranging precariousness that may well have engendered. In this explanation Johannes' inner unconscious hunger for security blinded him to the way the church could simultaneously protect him while suppressing the radical reach of his illumination.

A third explanation was suggested to me by the great Indologist, Alain Danielou, thirty-five years ago in Paris. He revered Angelus Silesius and we were speaking of the conundrum of his last years. "It may be," Alain said, "that Angelus Silesius simply could not bear the vast aloneness that a full awakening births you into, and desperately needed community, and paid a grotesque psychological price for it." He added, "If Angelus Silesius had had his awakening in the context of an ancient tolerant sacred culture such as medieval India, he would have been sustained and supported in a way impossible in the Christian world he lived in."

There is one more "explanation" which I include here for the sake of completeness and which was floated to me by an eccentric French-Canadian mystic poet who loved and constantly quoted Angelus Silesius. We were sitting together talking on the beach at Mahabalipuram in South India about the mystery of Silesius's fanaticism. He said, "Angelus Silesius was only pretending to be a fanatic Catholic. It was his way of protecting the outrageousness of his real vision from the authorities. What a brilliant way! Pretending to be a paid-up ferocious conformist so that no one could guess you were being transfigured and destroy the amazing masterpiece that showed that transfiguration is possible."

No one will ever know if any of these interpretations or explanations or a complex combination of them are true. The mystery of the strange journey of "Angelus Silesius" will always remain hidden.

In 1675, Johannes Angelus suddenly abandoned his polemical outbursts, withdrew into the cloister of St. Matthew Church in Breslau and started to give away all his money to the poor. After a mysterious illness, he died at 53 on the 9th of July, 1677.

The body of Johannes Angelus ("Angelus Silesius") was interred in St. Matthews Church, where 24 years earlier, he had first become a Catholic priest.

A BRIEF HISTORY OF THE RECEPTION OF THE CHERUBINIC PILGRIM

Although *The Cherubinic Pilgrim* was published under Catholic aegis, its warmest initial reception came from Lutheran Pietistic circles in Silesia, especially the one clustered around Gottfried Arnold, who in 1701 published a noteworthy edition. Pietism was a vast, amorphous Lutheran religious movement that opposed the increasingly sclerotic pragmatism of the reformed church.

In 1729, the pietist poet Gerhard Tersteegen imitated *The Cherubinic Pilgrim* in his most powerful opus, *Garden of the Spiritual Flowers of Fervent Souls*. After more than a half century of oblivion, *The Cherubinic Pilgrim*'s reputation was revived and expanded by enthusiastic romantic philosophers and poets. Hegel admired Silesius's paradoxical genius. Friedrich Schlegel wrote two seminal articles on his work in 1800 and 1809: both Schopenhauer and the great Danish mystic Kierkegaard praised Silesius in their recorded conversations and works. Profound spiritual poets like the Catholic Annette von Droste-Hülshoff and the orientalist Friedrich Rückert (beloved and immortalized by Mahler) embraced him. The greatest nineteenth century Swiss novelist Gottfried Keller worked a discussion of Silesius as well as a dozen of his epigrams into his masterpiece, *Green Henry* (*Der Grüne Heinrich*).

It wasn't until the modern period, however, that the universal power and mystical originality of *The Cherubinic Pilgrim* began to be celebrated. Heidegger commented complexly and dazzlingly on the couplet, "The Rose Without Why", in his *Principal of Reason*, one of the most provocative and influential of his works: Derrida wove quotations from Silesius into many of his cryptic, deconstructive texts; several of Europe's greatest modern visionary poets—the German Paul Celan, the French René Char, and the Englishman Geoffrey Hill—named Angelus Silesius as an essential precursor and inspiration of their own work. Fine translations into different European languages, such as those of the French scholar, Erik Sable, began to appear. On the last page of Umberto Eco's world best-seller, *The Name of the Rose* (1980), the aging narrator cites—without naming him—one of Silesius's most famous epigrams before concluding his masterpiece with a fugue of echoes from *The Cherubinic Pilgrim*.

Since Umberto Eco published *The Name of the Rose*, the reputation of Angelus Silesius as not only one of the great Christian mystic poets but, even more importantly, as one of a select group of universal mystic master poets—Rumi, Hafiz, Kabir—has continued to expand. As the lineaments of a universal mysticism start to emerge in response to our contemporary crisis, and as interest in embodied evolutionary mysticism—inspired by Aurobindo, Teilhard de Chardin, Bede Griffiths, among others—grows exponentially, *The Cherubinic Pilgrim* sings out to us in a fresh and astonishing way.

It is my prayer that *Becoming God* will bring Angelus Silesius as evolutionary pioneer and master of the Transfiguration Process to seekers on all paths.

Beloved Angelus Silesius
Be with us, in our long ordeal,
Inspire, ground, exalt, and ennoble us
As all outworn systems and dogmas burn
And the Age of the Great Birth begins.

Sanctus Sanctus Sanctus

ACKNOWLEDGEMENTS

To Jenny D'Angelo, for her brilliant editing and angelic companionship; to Ellen Gunter, great friend and superb writer; to Jill Angelo Birnbaum, for her loyalty and passion; to Miles Gunter, for all his strong kindness and wise help; to Jeff Brown, for his fierce courage and his great book, *Grounded Spirituality*; to Matt Fox, for his friendship and championing of Meister Eckhart, Hildegarde of Bingen, and now Angelus Silesius; to Mirabai Starr, our most eloquent translator of Christian mystics and a magnificent writer; to the great evolutionary pioneers, the Vedic sages, Pythagoras, Jesus, Kabir, Teilhard de Chardin, Bede Griffiths, the long lineage of Vajrayana Tibetan masters, the Kabbalists and others in all traditions who lived the secret of Transfiguration and kept its flame burning through long centuries of ignorance; and to Jade, my beloved cat, who continues to irradiate my life with her beauty and exquisite love.